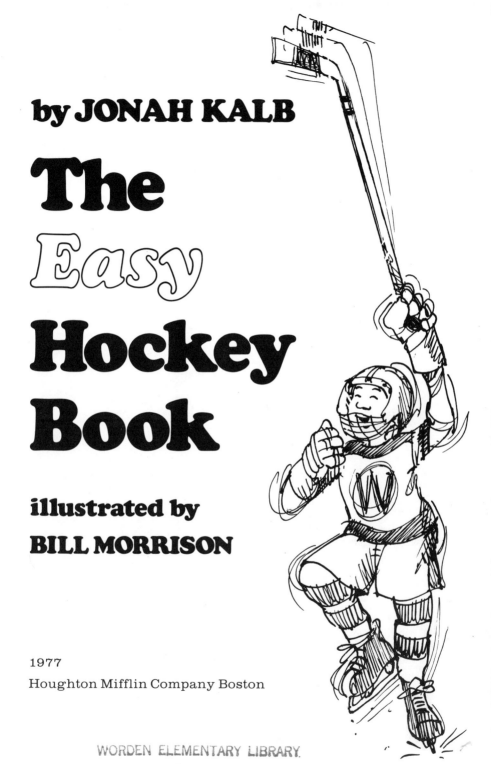

by JONAH KALB

The *Easy* Hockey Book

illustrated by
BILL MORRISON

1977

Houghton Mifflin Company Boston

To all the coaches of Squirts and Mites
and Peewees and Bantams who would be teaching
superstars, if only they had the ice time.

Also by JONAH KALB

The Easy Baseball Book
The Goof That Won the Pennant
The Kid's Candidate

By JONAH KALB and DAVID VISCOTT
What Every Kid Should Know

Library of Congress Cataloging in Publication Data

Kalb, Jonah.
   The easy hockey book.

   SUMMARY: An introduction for beginners to hockey,
including how to pass, stickhandle, skate, shoot,
obtain equipment, and sharpen skates.

   1. Hockey — Juvenile literature. [1. Hockey]
I. Morrison, Bill. II. Title.
GV847.25.K34   796.9'62   77-9917
ISBN 0-395-25842-1

Introduction

Playing ice hockey is very hard.

For one thing, the rink
is very big. It is the same size
for you as it is for the pros.

Also, you have to learn to skate
before you can even start to play.
That's like learning to ride a bike
before playing basketball.

Lastly, you have to be strong.
Even the pros get tired
after playing two or three minutes.

This book won't make the game easier.
It won't even teach you how to play.
You probably already know how to play.

But this book will give you details.
It will tell you some little things
that will help you skate better,
pass better, shoot better,

handle your stick better. It will tell
you things your coach would tell you
if he had the time.

If you love the game anyway,
even though it is a hard game to play,
this book is for you.

SKATING

Hockey is a skater's game.
You can't do anything in hockey
unless you skate well.

If you can, take figure skating lessons.
They are even better than hockey lessons.
Tell the teacher you are
a hockey player. Say you want to wear
your hockey skates.
The teacher won't mind.

Learn your skate edges.
Learn to skate backward.
Learn crossovers. Learn balance.
These are the best skills
a hockey player ever learns.

Skating Equipment

You probably already have hockey skates.
Make sure they fit properly.

Wiggle your toes. If you can't wiggle
them, or if the skates hurt your arches,
they are too small.

Step on the back of the blade of one
skate. Try to lift your heel inside
the boot. If you can lift it more
than one inch, the skates are too big.

You don't need new skates.
You need skates that fit.
You can buy used skates from other
players, and sell your old ones, too.

Keep your blades sharp.
Get them sharpened after three
or four hours on the ice.

You also need a helmet and hockey gloves.
Get a helmet with a plastic shield
to cover your face.
And get gloves that you can bend.

Never play hockey, even on a pond,
without your helmet and gloves.

Skating Forward

Hockey players almost always skate fast.
To start fast, take three or four running
steps on your toes. Then push, hard,
on the inside edge of your back skate.

Bend your forward knee.
Stretch to the full length
of your back leg on each stroke.
Keep your weight leaning forward.

And keep your head up.
You don't have to watch yourself skate.

Don't glide.
When one stroke is finished,
go right into the next stroke.

To stop, turn both skates sideways
to the path of your skating.
Keep your skates six inches apart.
Lean back. Push hard on the inside edge
of the lead skate and the outside edge
of the back skate. Dig into the ice.

Practice stopping left and right.
Hockey players who can't stop both ways
end up sitting on the bench.

Running start. Deep stroke. Bend knees.
Stretch back leg. Push hard. Weight
forward. Head up. Hockey stops both
sides.

Skating Backward

Backward skating is mostly gliding. You
"stroke" backward by wiggling your hips.

Start forward. Then, turn around.
Bend your knees.
Keep your feet about one foot apart.
Lean back enough to keep your rear
over the ice. Pump your arms. Wiggle.
Keep your head up.

As you wiggle your hips, push all you
can on the inside edges of one skate,
then the other.

The faster you wiggle, the faster you
skate, but nobody skates backward as fast
as he skates forward.

To stop, turn both skates outward.
Lean forward. Push hard and equally
on both inside edges. Dig into the ice.

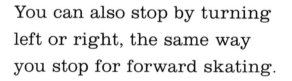

You can also stop by turning
left or right, the same way
you stop for forward skating.

Running forward start. Turn around.
Bend knees. Rear over the ice.
Feet apart. Glide. Wiggle. Head up.
Plow stop: point feet out; lean forward;
dig into ice. Or hockey stop,
left or right.

Turning

You must be able to turn both
left and right equally well.

To turn left, lead with your left skate.
Lean left. Bend your left knee.
Use the outside edge of your
left skate. You will also be
on the inside edge of your right skate.
Turn your left skate out. Glide.

To turn right, lead with your right skate.
Lean right. Bend your right knee.
Use the outside edge of your right skate.
Turn your right skate out. Keep your
shoulders level, even when you lean.

To turn more sharply,
you have to use crossovers.

You begin crossovers the same way.
Lead. Lean. Outside edge. Then,
lift your back skate over the front skate.
Push off. Lift again. Push again.

You must learn crossovers both sides,
left and right.

The secret to turning is leaning.
Don't worry about falling.
Everybody falls. Lean way over.

Common Skating Mistakes

Some players think they already know
how to skate. So they never practice.
Skating is like playing the piano.
You have to practice even after
you know how. Even pros practice.

Some players think they can shoot,
so skating isn't important.
They are wrong.

Some players learn to stop on one side.
If the puck goes to the other side,
they are helpless.

Some players never learn crossovers
on both sides.

Some beginners are afraid to fall.
Everybody falls. The best thing to do
is fall right away. Then you know
it doesn't hurt too much.

Some players don't lean enough.
Skating forward, lean forward. Turning,
lean into the turn. Shift your weight.

Some players skate, turn, or stop on the
flats of their blades. Blades have two
edges—inside and outside. Use them.

How to Practice Skating

AT THE RINK:

Skate forward. Glide around the
faceoff circle. Skate to the next circle.
Glide around again.

Do the same using crossovers. Do the
same going backward around the circles.

Put markers on the ice. Go inside one
and outside the other. Weave in and out.
Remember edges on your turns.

Do the same using crossovers. Do the
same going backward, in and out.

19

ON THE POND:

Play catch-up. Give someone a long lead
and then catch him.

Play tag. One person in the middle.
Anybody he tags also goes
in the middle. The last one left wins.

Race anybody who will race you.
Race backward.
Make teams and do relay races.

DURING THE SUMMER:

Run. Play tennis. Play baseball. Swim.
Have a good time. It all helps hockey.

STICKHANDLING

Most young hockey players stickhandle
too much. It looks good to the crowd,
but they end up losing the puck.
In most cases, it is better to pass
than to stickhandle.

Still, a player sometimes has to
carry the puck. He may have nobody
around him. He may be on his way
to the net. He may have open ice
before him.

So stickhandling is important.
But don't overdo it.

Stickhandling Equipment

Skates, helmet, and gloves. But also,
a puck and a hockey stick.

Pucks are pretty much the same.
Get an "official" weight and size.

Hockey sticks are different.
And you need the right kind for you.

Hockey sticks have curved blades.
Right-handed shooters and passers want
the inside of the curve facing forward
when the stick is on the right side.
Left-handed shooters and passers
want a stick curving the other way.

Right-handed people are not always
right-handed shooters and passers.
Try a friend's stick first. See if you
feel better shooting left or right.

Hockey sticks also have different "lies."
The "lie" is the angle between the blade
and the shaft. The number is printed on
the front of the shaft. Get a 5 or a 6.

Cut the shaft down to size. With the
blade between your feet, cut the shaft
so that it reaches your nose. Tape a knob
on the top. That will help you pick it up
off the ice, even when you are wearing
hockey gloves.

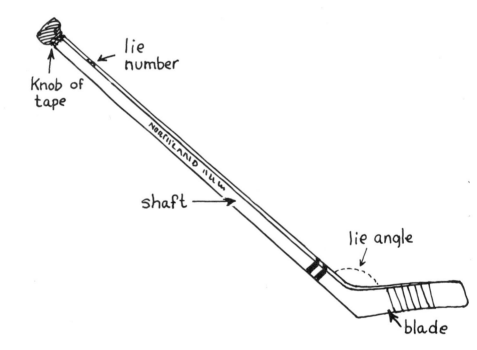

Carrying the Puck

Keep both hands on the stick.
If you are a right-handed shooter,
keep your left hand just under the knob.
Keep your right hand six inches lower.

Keep the puck well out in front of you.
If you do that, you can keep your head
up and look for the good pass. You will
also see your opponent. If you carry
the puck too close to your skates, you
will be looking down, and you might
get clobbered.

Keep the puck on your stick. Do not throw it ahead and then catch up. Control the puck by keeping it on the stick.

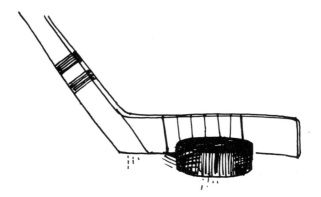

Carry the puck on the middle of your blade. You may sweep from your forehand to your backhand, but very small sweeps only. Most of the time you don't have to shift back and forth. Most of the time you just push the puck with your forehand. Sweeping back and forth is a good way to lose control of the puck.

Two hands on the stick. Puck well out in front. Head up. Sweep or push. If sweeping, small, gentle sweeps. Control the puck. Keep it on your stick.

Common Stickhandling Mistakes

Some players think they can stickhandle
a puck through a whole team of players.
They usually lose the puck.

Some players stickhandle with one hand.
In this case, an opponent usually lifts
his stick and takes the puck away.

Many players carry the puck too close
to their skates. They must look down
to find the puck and they often get hit.

Some players stickhandle with wide
sweeps. They forget that they are
supposed to be going forward.
They lose the puck a lot.

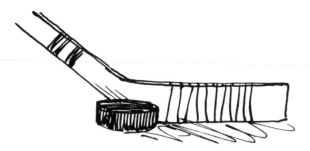

Some players carry the puck on the toe,
or the heel, of the blade. The puck
often just falls off.

Some players lift their sticks
off the ice when they stickhandle.
The puck goes underneath the blade.

Some players try to stickhandle
a rolling puck, or a spinning puck.
That is very, very hard to do.
Knock the puck flat, then carry it.

How to Practice Stickhandling

AT THE RINK:

Do all the practice drills in the
chapter on skating, but this time
use your stick and puck. Around the
circles, in and out of the markers,
up and down the ice.

Do it backward, dragging the puck.
Do it with crossovers.

Stickhandle up and down the ice
without ever looking at the puck.
Try to "feel" the puck on your stick.

ON THE POND:

Play keepaway. Keep the puck away
from one other player as long as you can.
No checking. Then, two players.
Then, three. See who can keep the puck
the longest.

Skate forward, stickhandling. Miss it on purpose. Then kick the puck back onto your stick with your skate.

DURING THE SUMMER:

Run. Play golf. Play street hockey. Play soccer. Stickhandle a ball on your driveway.

PASSING

Hockey is a team sport. Every team sport depends on passing.

Passing is also what makes hockey such a fast game. Skating and passing. The puck moves faster when you are passing.

Passing isn't "throwing." Passing means getting the puck to somebody on your own team.

That would be simple if everybody were standing still. But the passer is usually moving. And the receiver is usually moving. So passing takes some skill.

And practice.

Passing Equipment

Passing equipment is the same as the equipment you need for stickhandling: skates, helmet, gloves, puck, stick.

But you will need other equipment before you can play hockey safely.

You will need shin pads, and they must be the right size. If they are too big, or too small, they will bother your skating.

Boys will need an athletic supporter with a plastic cup.

You will need shoulder pads and elbow pads. You will need padded hockey pants to protect your thighs, hips, and kidneys.

You will need hockey stockings that go over your shin pads and a garter belt to hold them up.

You will need suspenders to hold up your hockey pants.

You will need an inside mouth guard that goes over your teeth. And you will need an outside mouth guard to protect your lips.

You will need a chin strap with a guard that holds your helmet and protects your chin.

shin pads

athletic supporter

cup

shoulder pads

elbow pads

inside and outside mouth guards

Passing from the Forehand

Most passes are from the forehand.

For a right-handed passer, the stick is held as in stickhandling — left hand under the knob, right hand six inches or so below.

Stand, or skate, sideways to the direction of the pass, feet apart. Start with the puck one foot behind your back skate, on the middle of your stick blade. Look up at your receiver.

Sweep — do not hit — sweep the puck across your body in the direction of your receiver. Shift your weight from the back to the front skate, with the puck.

Follow through. End up pointing your stick toward the puck.

If the receiver is skating, you must
lead the receiver. Pass it to where
he will be when the puck gets there.

Lead your receiver more than you think
you should. Try to get the puck to his
stick. Remember, his stick is three feet in
front.

The best passes are "crisp." Not so
hard that your receiver can't catch.
Not so soft that anybody can intercept.

Passing from the Backhand

Passing from the backhand is almost like passing from the forehand, except it is harder to do.

It is harder because you are passing from the outside of the curve on your blade. Also, your lower hand is pulling the stick, instead of pushing it.

Still, you have to learn the backhand pass.

Drop your lower hand another six inches.
Keep the puck near your back skate.
Stand sideways to the path of your pass.
Look up. Sweep the puck.
Follow through. Let your weight follow the puck from your back skate to your front skate.

Most backhand passes are short. If you need a long pass, try to make it with your forehand.

Lead your receiver. If he is skating forward, lead him more than you think you should. If you lead him too much, the puck will go into your opponent's end, and that's not too bad. But if you put it in his skates, he must stop. Someone will probably beat him to the puck.

Receiving a Pass

Keep your stick on the ice.
Keep both hands on your stick.

If you keep your stick on the ice,
the passer knows you are ready
to catch his pass. He has a target.

In catching a pass, keep your eyes on the
puck all the way to your stick. Watch the
puck hit the stick.

When the puck hits your blade, loosen
your bottom hand. Hold your top hand
tight. The stick will "give" a little,
and will not let the puck bounce off.
Catch the puck in the middle of your
blade.

If the pass is behind you, you have to
stop and get it. If the pass is in your
skates, stop it with your skates and try
to kick it up to your stick.

If the puck is too far ahead of you,
skate as fast as you can and get it.

Assume a good pass. Don't slow down
until you know the puck is behind you.

"Give" a little when you receive. And
keep your stick on the ice.

Common Passing Mistakes

Some players slap at the puck, or hit it.
Sweep the puck, like sweeping a floor.

Some players wait too long before
passing. They forget that their opponent
also has a stick.
That makes the opponent's reach longer.

Some players lift their heads just as
the puck reaches them. They often miss
the pass. Watch the puck all the way to
your blade.

Some players don't look before they
pass. Remember, you must pass the puck
to somebody.

Some players just don't pass hard enough.
"Crisp" passing is best.

Many players do not lead a moving skater
far enough. The puck ends up in the
receiver's skates. Aim for the stick!

Some players try to pass, or try to
receive, with only one hand on the stick.

Believe it or not, some players do not
keep their sticks on the ice.

How to Practice Passing

AT THE RINK:

Put a marker on the ice. Stickhandle
with a puck. Then pass to the marker.
See how often you can hit the marker.

Skate up and down the ice with another
player, passing the puck back and forth.
See if you can go up and down the length
of the rink without even one bad pass.

Stand by the net. Pass to a player
skating as fast as he can up the boards.

Pass to yourself by bouncing passes
off the boards. See if you can go
all the way up and down without ever
slowing down.

ON THE POND:

Pass back and forth with a friend.

Pass to a tree stump after
stickhandling. Practice kicking the
puck up to your stick.

Practice leading.
Practice backhand passes.

DURING THE SUMMER:

Throw a football to a friend.
Practice leading.
You will have to lead more in hockey.

SHOOTING

For most young players, shooting is the best part of hockey. After all, that is all they count at the end – the number of goals.

In youth hockey, half the goals will be scored by pushing, or little flip shots, from right in front of the net.

Almost all the rest of the goals will be scored by wrist shots on breakaways, or two on ones.

That means everybody should practice flip shots and wrist shots every time they get on the ice.

So why do so many young players spend all their practice time on their slap shots?

Shooting Equipment

To shoot, you need a stick and a puck.
That means you wear your skates and
gloves. If you wear your skates, you wear
your helmet. And if anybody else
is on the ice, you wear your inside and
outside mouthpiece. If there is a game,
you wear everything.

Be sure to wear a helmet with a plastic
face visor to protect your eyes.
Eye injuries are very serious.

Some players wear cages instead of
plastic face guards. Cages are
better than nothing, but not as good
as plastic visors.

The only other equipment you need
for shooting is a goal net.

The Wrist Shot

The wrist shot is the basic shot
in hockey. You can aim it.
You can shoot it hard.
You can get it off quickly.

If you are a right-handed shooter,
face the puck, standing sideways to the
net, just like a golfer facing the ball.
Keep your feet apart. Bend your knees.
Drop your bottom hand as low as you can
without feeling uncomfortable.

The puck should be a foot behind your
back skate. Cock your wrists. Look at
the net. Then look back at the puck.
Sweep the puck as hard as you can
toward the net.

Shift your weight forward as the puck
moves forward. Keep your head over
the puck. When it reaches your front
skate, explode your wrists, and roll
them under the stick.

Follow through. If you want the shot
high, follow through high. If you want

it low, follow through low. The blade should be pointing face up.

Backhand wrist shots are done the same way, but drop your bottom hand still lower.

Left-handed shooters do the same thing with opposite hands and feet.

The Flip Shot

There is a scramble in front of the net. The goalie goes down. The puck is kicked out right on your stick, because your stick was on the ice.
What do you do?

You flip the puck into the top part of the net. Then, everybody cheers.

The flip shot is made with very little power. And you should never flip from

more than ten feet. If you are farther
out, wrist-shoot.

Don't bother setting your feet. Get
the puck on the toe of your blade, near
the end. Scoop under it. Pretend you
want to pick the puck up with your
blade and hand it to somebody. Scoop.
Flip with your wrists. Lift it up.

Backhand flips are much harder because
the stick is curved the wrong way. Flip
those from the heel of your blade,
near the shaft. Place your bottom hand
very low.

The flip shot works because the goalie
is down. So do it quickly, before he
gets up.

The Slap Shot

The best thing about a slap shot
is its power. Even if the goalie
stops it, he may leave a rebound.

But the slap shot takes a lot of time.
Often the puck is stolen while the
shooter winds up.

And it is a very hard shot to aim.
Even the pros can put only half
their slap shots on net. Nobody
ever scored by shooting and missing
the net.

The shot is very much like the wrist shot,
except the puck should be lying still,
about halfway between your feet.

Instead of sweeping, you raise your
stick something like a golfer. But
don't raise it higher than your shoulder.
Position your low hand really low —
as low as you can manage.

Look at the net. Look at the puck. Cock your wrists. Then swing, as hard as you can, for the back of the puck. Let your weight go all the way forward as you swing. Explode your wrists at impact. Follow through. Pray.

When and Where to Shoot

Quick shots are better than windups. Shooting when the goalie isn't expecting you to shoot is best.

Shoot on net. The goal is four feet high, six feet wide. That's big enough.

If you can, shoot where the goalie isn't.
If he is on the left side, shoot for the
right. If he is down, shoot high.

If he is standing, in good position,
shooting low is better than shooting
high. Goalies, with all those pads, do
not move their feet as fast as they
move their hands.

If shooting high anyway, shoot for over
the stick hand, not the glove hand. At
least make him drag that heavy stick up.

Hard shots on the ice leave more
rebounds than hard shots in the air.

If you have the shot, take it. Don't
pass if you have a clear shot, even if
your teammate is nearer. Take the shot
yourself. Your teammate may miss the
pass. Also, just because he's closer
doesn't mean he has an opening.

Common Shooting Mistakes

Some players wait too long before shooting. If you have the shot, shoot. Quickly. Before the goalie gets back into position.

In scrambles in front of the net, many players just shove the puck back into the pack. Flip the puck over the goalie. Get it in the air.

Some players don't move their weight forward as they shoot. They wrist-shoot, and even slap-shoot off their back skates. The weight should move forward with the puck.

Some players don't follow through. Follow high for a high shot, low for a low shot. But follow the puck.

Some players don't lower their back

hand before shooting. The low hand gives power. The lower, the better. Very low for slap shots.

Some players don't cock their wrists before shooting, or don't explode their wrists on contact. They lose power.

Some slap shooters think that when the crowd ooohs and aaahs, they have scored a goal. Only when the puck goes into the net is a goal scored.

Many players practice only their slap shots.

How to Practice Shooting

AT THE RINK:

The only way to practice shooting is to shoot. Line up pucks on the blue line and wrist-shoot them into the net. Line up pucks in a 10-foot circle and flip-shoot them into the net.

Start at the red line. Skate forward fast and wrist-shoot into the net. Try different angles. Try backhanders.

Block off the bottom of the net with
goalie pads, or orange crates,
or markers. Wrist-shoot into the net,
over the obstacle.

Shoot the puck to the boards.
Wherever the rebound comes,
wrist-shoot for the net.

Once in a great while,
practice your slap shot.

ON THE POND:

Be careful. Use only the area marked
for hockey players. Do all the above.

DURING THE SUMMER:

If your parents let you, mark off a net
on the garage wall — four feet high,
six feet wide. Get a large piece of
plywood. Wax it. Shoot regular hockey
pucks off the plywood at the wall.

Play baseball. Play golf. Play tennis.
Play.

When a goal is scored by your team,
hold your stick high in the air.
Hold it straight up.
Smile. Laugh. Dance a little.

Put your other arm up, too.
Hug any player from your team.
Hit your goalie on his pads
with your stick.

None of this is in the rulebook.
But it is a tradition
as old as the game itself.

Such total joy
is what the game is all about.